AUSTRALIA'S REMARKABLE WILDLIFE

JOHN LESLEY

QUOKKA

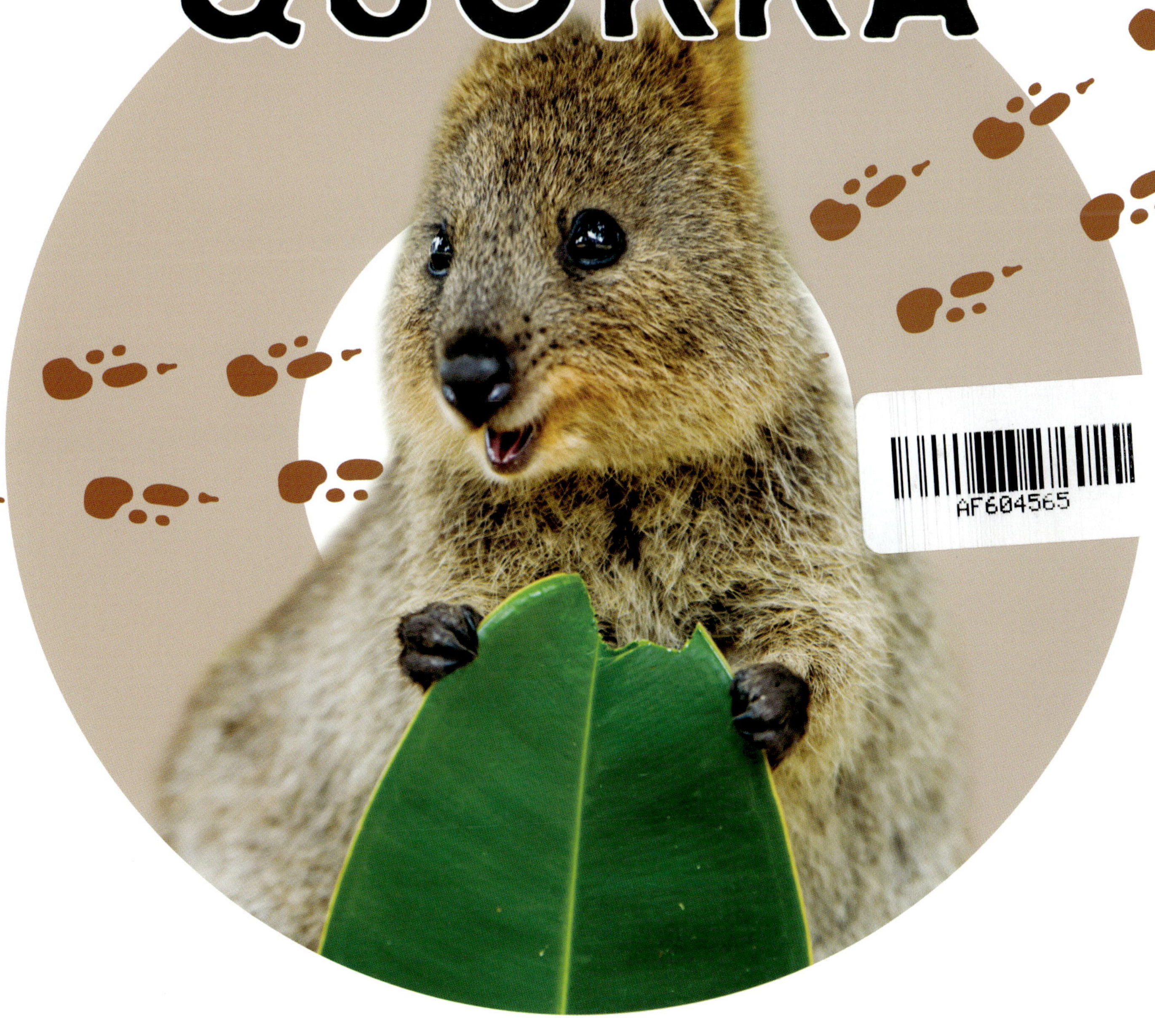

REDBACK publishing

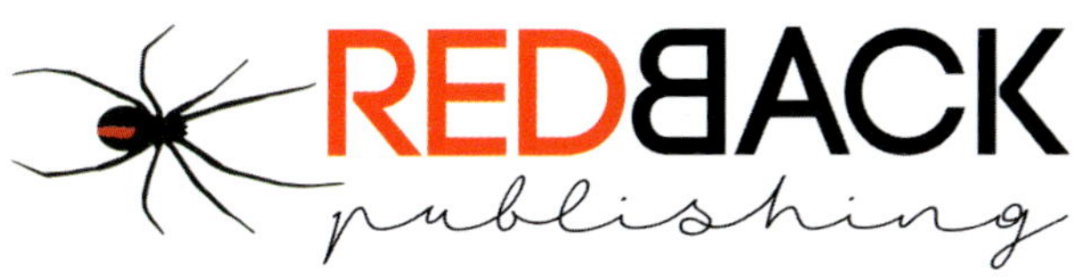

First Published 2025 by
Redback Publishing
Suite 6, 13a Narabang Way,
Belrose NSW 2085
Australia

www.redbackpublishing.com
orders@redbackpublishing.com

ISBN 978-1-761400-17-9 PBK

Author: John Lesley
Editor: Caroline Thomas
Design: Redback Publishing

A catalogue record for this book is available from the National Library of Australia

Original illustrations © Redback Publishing 2025
Originated by Redback Publishing

Printed and bound in Malaysia

Acknowledgements
Abbreviations: l—left, r—right, b—bottom, t—top, c—centre, m—middle
We would like to thank the following for permission to reproduce photographs: (Images © shutterstock) p25tl Osprey Creative / Shutterstock.com

CONTENTS

QUOKKA

Quokkas have strong hind legs for hopping.

Quokkas have small claws for climbing trees and holding food.

Quokka babies are called joeys. They begin life in their mother's pouch.

Joey in pouch

QUOKKA BASIC FACTS

FUR

Quokkas have thick, coarse fur that is brownish grey, and lighter underneath on the chest and belly. The tail does not have fur, but fur does grow close to the claws.

APPEARANCE

Quokkas grow to about half a metre long and they have a thin tail. An adult may weigh about four kilograms.

They have rounded, furry ears and a short head. The front limbs are used to pick up food and for climbing bushes, where they find some of their food, and where they can protect themselves from danger. The hind limbs are larger and stronger, for running and hopping.

NAME

The word quokka is from the Noongar name for the animal, which is quak-a.

Quokkas are marsupials and native Australian wallabies. Like all marsupials, the mother quokka carries her baby in a pouch, and feeds it on milk she produces. There is only one type of quokka alive today. Its scientific name is *Setonix brachyurus*.

QUOKKA HISTORY

MILLIONS OF YEARS AGO

THOUSANDS OF YEARS AGO

10,000 YEARS AGO

1658

Millions of years ago

Quokkas have existed in the southwest of Australia for millions of years, long before any human beings were around.

Thousands of years ago

The Noongar Indigenous people named the quokka. The place now known as Rottnest Island was an important ceremonial site for the Noongar people.

10,000 years ago

Rottnest Island was once joined to the mainland by dry land. Rising sea levels at the end of the last Ice Age isolated the quokkas that were living on Rottnest Island.

1658

A Dutch sailor saw the quokkas and wrote that they were some kind of cat. This was probably the first record made by a European person of an Australian animal.

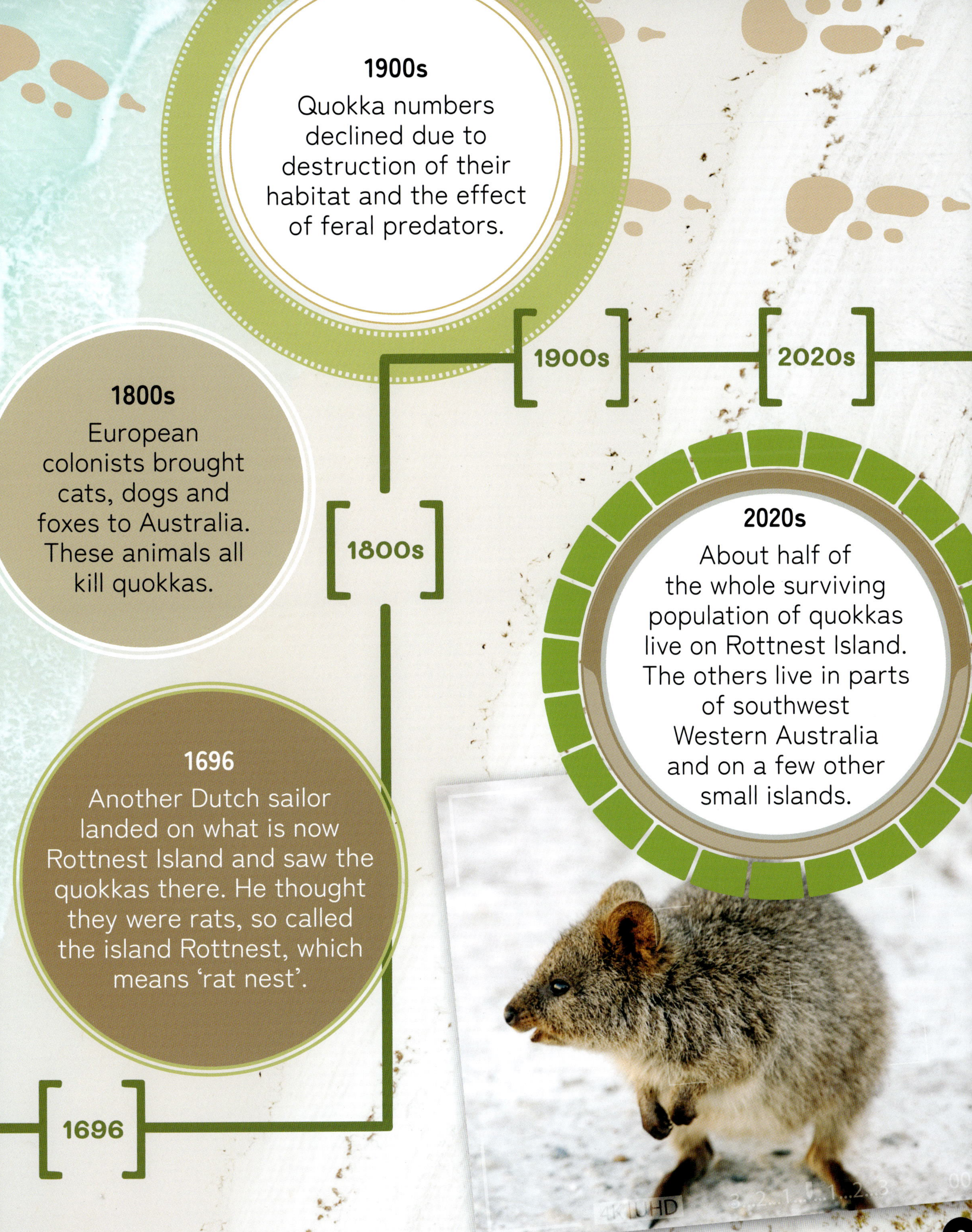
1900s
Quokka numbers declined due to destruction of their habitat and the effect of feral predators.
1900s
2020s
1800s
European colonists brought cats, dogs and foxes to Australia. These animals all kill quokkas.
1800s
2020s
About half of the whole surviving population of quokkas live on Rottnest Island. The others live in parts of southwest Western Australia and on a few other small islands.
1696
Another Dutch sailor landed on what is now Rottnest Island and saw the quokkas there. He thought they were rats, so called the island Rottnest, which means 'rat nest'.
1696

QUOKKA ADAPTATIONS

Quokkas have been able to slowly evolve over millions of years, resulting in them being adapted to their environment.

Their brownish grey fur is the same colour as dry grass, so it camouflages quokkas from predators.

Quokkas are nocturnal. At night, they can hide more easily from predators, and they can also escape from the heat by not being active in the hottest parts of the day.

Quokkas are adapted to living in a hot, dry climate. They can go for long periods with very little water to drink.

Quokkas front claws are very useful. They can pick up food with them, and use them to climb bushes to reach leaves to eat.

From 1788 onwards, settlers started arriving in Australia from other parts of the world, bringing their feral animals with them. This had a negative effect on quokka survival.

Despite being perfectly adapted to their environment before this happened, quokkas have not had enough time to adapt to these new changes. Declining numbers of quokkas have been the result.

Visitors to Rottnest Island encourage quokkas to come out in the daytime by offering them food. This can upset the quokkas' natural behaviour patterns.

QUOKKA HABITAT

Quokkas live in southwest Western Australia. There are a few on the mainland, but the largest population is on Rottnest Island, where about 10,000 quokkas form a major tourist attraction.

They live amongst dense shrubs, and look for food along beaches, near rivers and lakes, and in forests. On Rottnest Island, they also visit the town area, looking for food scraps.

Quokkas create pathways through thick grass and shrubs. These paths are used to travel around their habitat, and as escape routes from predators.

QUOKKA LIFE CYCLE

A quokka baby is called a joey. Like all marsupials, quokka mothers give birth to a tiny, underdeveloped baby. After it is born, the joey crawls into the pouch and begins feeding on its mother's milk. The joey stays with its mother until it is about eight months old.

Baby quokka

At eighteen months old, a female quokka will mate and start producing offspring. The mother produces one or two joeys each year.

Quokkas live either alone or in small groups. They can live for about ten years in the wild.

QUOKKA FOOD CHAIN

WHAT DOES A QUOKKA EAT?

Quokkas eat grasses, seeds, leaves and plant roots. On Rottnest Island they have been observed occasionally eating insects and worms. This is usually only during the breeding season, when the female needs more protein to produce and feed the joey.

WHAT EATS QUOKKAS?

Predators of quokkas include feral cats, foxes and dogs, as well as dingoes. Eagles may take the baby quokkas.

Dingo

SAFETY FOR QUOKKAS ON ROTTNEST ISLAND

Fortunately, there are no foxes or dingoes on Rottnest Island. These two animals hunt and eat quokkas, and contributed to reducing quokka numbers on the Western Australian mainland.

WHERE TO SEE A QUOKKA

Tourists have the best chance of seeing quokkas in the wild on Rottnest Island, off the Western Australian coast. Some quokkas live on the mainland, but they are more timid, and not as easy to find and observe.

Most Australian zoos have quokkas on display. Zoos play an important role in helping to ensure the quokka does not become extinct. Having quokka breeding programs at zoos is one of the ways that people can try to stop quokkas from dying out.

A FEW BASIC RULES

If you are lucky enough to visit Rottnest Island, there are a few rules you must follow when meeting a quokka:

- Let the quokka come up to you
- Do not chase it
- Do not feed it
- Do not touch it

Quokkas are protected in Australia and very strong penalties apply if they are harmed or taken from their habitat.

YES, THEY BITE!

An annoyed quokka will certainly bite you. They also bite each other if they get into a fight.

THE FUTURE OF QUOKKAS

The IUCN Red List of Threatened Species is an international list of the world's threatened animals, fungi and plants. It lists the quokka as VU (vulnerable), meaning its continued existence is under threat.

There are only about 12,000 adult quokkas left alive, and they live in a relatively small area of Western Australia, on the mainland and on some nearby islands. The baiting of foxes with poison will help to protect the quokka. Ensuring its forest habitat is not totally destroyed is also a very important way that quokkas can be protected.

Wildlife carer nursing a quokka

PEOPLE AND QUOKKAS

There were once many thousands of quokkas on the mainland of southern Western Australia, as well as on the islands not far from the shore.

Quokka numbers are now much reduced, due to the destruction of their habitat and feral predators such as foxes, dogs and cats.

People who feed quokkas human food are not helping. This sort of food makes them thirsty and sick.

Unlike most wild animals, quokkas will often come up to humans and investigate them. This fearlessness means that quokkas are often found near the settlement on Rottnest Island, where they can be run over by vehicles on the roads.

SOCIAL MEDIA

IS SOCIAL MEDIA GOOD OR BAD FOR QUOKKAS?

Social media has had both a positive and a negative effect on quokka numbers. Cute posts have brought the quokka to the attention of people worldwide, highlighting the animal's endangered status. However, the social media photos were so charming that thousands of people now visit Rottnest Island just to see a wild quokka.

RULES FOR QUOKKA SELFIES

Every tourist to Rottnest Island goes there to take a 'selfie' with a quokka. While the quokkas are used to this, there are a few important rules to follow:

- Remember that quokkas are wild animals
- You are not allowed to touch or feed them
- Using a 'selfie stick' will help to keep you at a distance from the quokka you are photographing

QUOKKA QUESTIONS AND ANSWERS

Q.

Why do quokkas smile?

A.

A quokka looks as though it is smiling, which delights anyone who sees it. Of course, it is not really smiling, and the upturned corners of the mouth are always there.

Q.

Can I have a pet quokka?

A.

As with all Australian native wildlife, it is illegal to keep a quokka as a pet. Zoos and wildlife carers need special permission to keep quokkas in Australia.

Although the quokkas on Rottnest Island are very tame, it is illegal for anyone to feed them or touch them.

So, no you cannot have one as a pet!

SORTING ANIMALS INTO GROUPS

Biologists divide all living things around the world into groups. They call this process classification.

The two basic groups of animals are called:

- **vertebrates** (with a backbone)
- **invertebrates** (without a backbone)

Quokkas are vertebrates. They are also marsupial mammals, a group which includes kangaroos, koalas and wombats. Most of the world's marsupials live in Australia.

Kangaroo

Koala

Wombat

CHARACTERISTICS OF MARSUPIAL MAMMALS

They give birth to very underdeveloped babies

They are warm-blooded

The baby then usually grows inside its mother's pouch

They are covered in hair

The female produces milk to feed her baby as it is developing

The baby marsupial is usually called a joey

GLOSSARY

baiting leaving poison in an area for an animal to eat

breeding season time of the year when an animal group produces its offspring

camouflage (verb) enable something to be hidden using its shape or colour

evolve change slowly over time to adapt to an environment

feral not being native to an area

joey baby marsupial

mainland large area of land near small islands

marsupial type of mammal that usually has a pouch to carry its babies

mate (verb) when a male and female come together to produce offspring

nocturnal being active at night

predator animal that hunts another for food

route pathway that is used often to get from one place to another

selfie photo taken of oneself, usually for posting to social media

INDEX